T0129839

# WHAT BEGINS WITH
# LOVE ENDS WITH JOY

Donald L. Brush, III

authorHOUSE®

*AuthorHouse™*
*1663 Liberty Drive*
*Bloomington, IN 47403*
*www.authorhouse.com*
*Phone: 1 (800) 839-8640*

*Published by AuthorHouse  02/14/2019*

*ISBN: 978-1-5462-7456-8 (sc)*
*ISBN: 978-1-5462-7459-9 (e)*

*Print information available on the last page.*

*Any people depicted in stock imagery provided by Getty Images are models, and such images are being used for illustrative purposes only. Certain stock imagery © Getty Images.*

*This book is printed on acid-free paper.*

*Scripture taken from The Holy Bible, King James Version. Public Domain*

*Scripture quotations marked NIV are taken from the Holy Bible, New International Version®. NIV®. Copyright © 1973, 1978, 1984 by International Bible Society. Used by permission of Zondervan. All rights reserved. [Biblica]*

*Scripture quotations marked TLB are taken from The Living Bible copyright © 1971. Used by permission of Tyndale House Publishers, Inc., Carol Stream, Illinois 60188. All rights reserved.*

*Scripture quotations marked NKJV are taken from the New King James Version. Copyright © 1982 by Thomas Nelson, Inc. Used by permission. All rights reserved.*

*The Living Bible copyright © 1971 by Tyndale House Foundation. Used by permission of Tyndale House Publishers Inc., Carol Stream, Illinois 60188. All rights reserved. The Living Bible, TLB, and the The Living Bible logo are registered trademarks of Tyndale House Publishers.*

*Scripture quotations marked NLT are taken from the Holy Bible, New Living Translation, copyright © 1996, 2004, 2007. Used by permission of Tyndale House Publishers, Inc. Carol Stream, Illinois 60188. All rights reserved. Website*

# INTRODUCING THE AUTHOR

Please share with me the pleasure of introducing to you my nephew Donald L. Brush, III, who has lived in the Suwanee Correctional Institution for almost ten years, enduring a life sentence without parole. Because of the invasion of the Spirit, Don is a new person not living under the shadow of confinement, loneliness, and morbidity any more; rather his focus is on the Godly walk, cultivated by active closeness to the Chapel services, the Bible studies led by dedicated and spiritually intense clergy, prayer groups centered on the concerns of the inmate community, plus I must add the A.A.'s Twelve Steps, the Serenity Prayer, and the life-changing, God-centered, resources of being "A friend of Bill."

In these pages you will find that Don uses art, poetry and stories as a lively way of giving expression to his faith. Should you want your own spirit to come to life, read on.

Spread joy!

The Rev. Dr. Stuart C. Brush
Woodbury, CT
Uncle of Donald III

# CREDITS

Mr. Brush uses an approach in the writing of very personal traits. The result is very enlightening as well as thought inducing. I sincerely recommend anyone to both read and enjoy a truly uplifting experience, a feast.

A proof reader for this book, and other writings of D. L. Brush

--Scott T. Foh

It is with pleasure that I write the following statement regarding "What Begins with Love, Ends with Joy ," and its author, Donald L. Brush. It is a work of Love. The Faith of Mr. Brush allows him to grant Forgiveness, have Patience and Humility. His Honesty is apparent with his Kindness and shows great Integrity. Mr. Brush's Wisdom has given him Peace. His Generosity grants him much Joy. I recommend readers the same levels and allow them to witness how words can become actions.

Sincerely, Dr. David Broxterman, PHDT,

United States Army, Retired

# FOREWORD

Most people have one or more gifts that make them unique in the virtues of life. This booklet has twelve virtues that work together to give God's children a description on how God wants us to live together in today's society.

My hope is that this booklet will be an encouragement to help us all live so that our lives will encourage others to live according to God's will.

Each chapter will break down an individual virtue that will help you to live your life in a way that will please God. Practicing these virtues will show others that you are a child of God.

What you are about to read is a collection of virtues that align with God's word. My prayer is that the reader can see God's plan for living a righteous life. I created this book to inspire and encourage people to live according to God's commandments.

I created this inspirational booklet because of the encouragement that I received from my Uncle, The God loving Rev. Dr. Stuart C. Brush. His message to me in his letters is to 'Spread Joy'. This is my way to spread joy as well as spreading God's word.

May this booklet draw you closer to the Lord. May He pour His blessings down upon you as you put these virtues to work in your lives.

Respectfully Submitted
Donald L. Brush III

# "Love"

One of God's greatest attributes is love. Love is the description of who God is, and how He feels about us. God commands that we love Him and one another. It is through us loving Him that we discover how much we are loved by Him.

(1 John 4:7-8) (NIV) "Dear friends, let us love one another, for love comes from God. Everyone who has love has been born of God. Whoever does not love, does not know God, because God is love."

God gives us faith as a means of getting in touch with His love. That enables us to pass on His love to others. God does not want us to hoard His love. He desires that we pass on His love to others. By spreading His love and joy, we improve the lives of others around us.

Love is not a warm and fuzzy feeling. It's an attitude and a decision to put another's interests above our own. True love is not based on outer appearance. It goes much deeper and is a matter of the heart. Sometimes love is tested to see if it is real. It is always inspiring when someone passes the test.

We are naturally drawn to beautiful and loving people. Mature love knows how to love those who seem so unlovable, those who are incapable of giving love in return for our love. This kind of love is from Heaven. God stretches our hearts capacity when He tells us to love our enemies. Loving them proves that we belong to God, for He loves everyone, no matter what they have done.

It's better to have loved and lost, than never to have loved at all. When we grieve for lost loved ones, we tend to grieve ourselves. Let us celebrate that those who have gone home to Heaven now know the fullest essence of God's true love.

We do not naturally love like God loves, but we can desire to grow in love, by demonstrating God's love to others. Even though we may call ourselves loving, we often justify a negative action by saying, "He deserved that." When someone comes against us with evil intentions and we respond with goodness, we are showing love.

Real love brings out the best in us. To show others love, will show others that you are capable of being loved. (John 15:13) (KJV) "Greater love has no man than this, that a man lay down his life for his friends."

(1 Corinthians 13:4-7) (NIV) "Love is patient, love is kind. It does not envy, it does not boast, it is not proud. It does not dishonor others, it is not self-seeking, it is not easily angered, it keeps no record of wrongs. Love does not delight in evil but rejoices with the truth. It always trusts, always hopes, always perserves."

# "Faith"

To have faith is to believe, to trust, to have confidence in, or to rely on something or someone. Faithfulness describes the quality of someone who will keep a promise or an oath to keep their word. God is our example of faith and faithfulness. He has kept every promise contained in the scriptures. God has commanded us to "Have faith in God," and out of our faith in Him, we remain faithful.

It is not a question in any of us having faith or not having faith; the question lies in what or who to have faith in. Faith never knows where it's being led, but it loves and knows the one who is leading. Faith thrives when we keep our focus on God and not on ourselves.

Faith sometimes means giving back to God the people or things we cherish most. The man Abraham was tested, and his response has become the model of faith for all believers. If our faith never gets tested; how would we know we had any? When things in our lives go wrong, as they often do, and we can say still, "I have faith in God, no matter what happens," then we show that our faith is real.

When a task comes before us, requiring faith, voices around us may say, "It can't be done." That voice may even come from inside each one of us. We may feel as if we ought to quit before we even get started. But if we just hold on to our faith, and believe in ourselves, we can succeed, no matter that voice may say.

Sometimes a person doesn't have much faith in himself or in anyone else. But a loved one's faith may be just enough to fill on the pathway He has chosen for us. Forgiveness is not dependent on our feelings, but it is rather our determination to follow His will. A few well chosen words of forgiveness are like an antiseptic that cleanses the wound and promotes healing.

The biblical story of the prodigal son reminds us that God is eager to forgive us and it prompts us to be ready to forgive others. (2 Corinthians 2:7) (NIV) "Now instead, you ought to forgive and comfort him; so that he will not be overwhelmed with sorrow." Only by calling on God are we able to forgive and forget!

Even if we feel that we have been wronged by someone, if we soften our hearts and forgive, the burden of bitterness will be lifted. The change is certain to affect the lives of those around us. Sometimes it may seem impossible to forgive other people, especially it they are purposely trying to hurt us. But if Jesus could forgive the people who crucified Him, certainly we can forgive the people who hurt us. That would show God's perfect love!

(Ephesians 4:32) (KJV) "Be kind to one another, tenderhearted, forgiving one another as God in Christ has forgiven you!" Forgive one another. Resentment is an unhealthy relationship of emotions.

# "Patience"

Throughout life, one of the hardest words to hear is 'Wait'. Sometimes we may anxiously wonder, 'Where is God when we need Him?' And yet we are reminded in the scriptures, (Isaiah 30:18) (KJV) "Blessed are all those who wait for Him to help them." Patience is developed through faithfully waiting. As we learn and understand patience, we will also learn to trust that God has our best interests in mind.

Waiting, endless waiting. Why does it seem so impossible to wait patiently? Throughout life, people tell us, 'Patience is a virtue.' Yet many people have trouble with that concept. Many people find it most difficult to attain and practice patience.

We may need to endure hard times, but we can trust that whatever happens, it is part of God's plan. The trials that come into our lives are the opportunity through which we learn patience.

We often need to patiently endure time and experience, in order to be fully prepared for whatever God has planned for our lives. Moses spent eight years preparing for the commission God gave him. (Proverbs 14:29) (KJV) "A patient man has great understanding, but a quick tempered man displays folly."

A great work of art takes time to be perfected in the hands of the artist. Even a clay pot maker takes time to mold the perfect planter. You've heard you can't rush perfection. Patience is time, after all, one thing we all have is time. Young children may ask, "Are we there yet?" The parents most used response is, "Be patient, we'll be there soon.

One of the Bible's all time favorite stories is that of the great flood. Besides being a wonderful story, it also provides valuable lessons about patience and faith. What patience Noah showed. During those long years of labor, long months of confinement, he did not complain. He waited. The key to patience is waiting.

(Romans 8:28) (KJV) "And we know that all things work together for good to them that love the Lord, to them who are called according to His purpose." And, (Romans 12:12) (TLB) "Be glad for all God is planning for you. Be patient in trouble, and always be prayerful." (Isaiah 40:31) (KJV) "But they that wait on the Lord shall renew their strength; they shall mount up with wings as eagles, they shall run and not be weary; and they shall walk, and not faint."

Good things come to those who wait. Be patient, your time will come. Don't rush time, it will end soon enough. Be patient, God will move in your life in His time. If you are patient with others, others will be patient with you!

# "Humility"

Most of us find that we are naturally self-centered. That we often respond to others around us in a manner that makes us appear proud. But if we look at the way Jesus lived, we see a perfect example of how God wants us to live. Rather than flaunt His own greatness, Jesus was willing to kneel down and wash the feet of others, to show us that we should all be servants for one another, and to God.

Contentment as well as usefulness, comes as a result of humbleness. (Micah 6:8) (NIV) "He has shown you, O mortal, what is good. And what does the Lord require of you? To act justly and to love mercy and to walk humbly with your God."

(1 Peter 5:5-6) (NIV) "In the same way, you who are younger, submit yourselves to your elders. All of you, clothe yourselves with humility toward one another, because, God opposes the proud but shows favor to the humble. Humble yourselves, therefore, under God's mighty hand, that He may lift you up in due time." (Psalm 37:11) (KJV) "But the meek (humble) shall inherit the earth, and shall delight themselves in the abundance of peace."

Like a multi-faceted gemstone, the humble person's color shimmers and shines forth. By their nature, they are able to bear an injustice without retaliating, do one's duty even when no one is watching, keep at the job until finished, and make use of criticism without being defeated by it.

Sometimes the best way to humble ourselves is just to walk outside and see the wonders God has made. A daily walk provides a peaceful way to focus on the world outside ourselves. Only a life of prayer can help the believer arrive at a spirit of humility, meekness and Christlikeness.

Rather than proudly striving to get ahead on our own, we must learn to relax with what God has provided for all of us. Only this will bring us

God's perfect rest. Christ was the perfect example of what being humble really means. While it may be difficult, we should make every effort to follow His example of humility.

The Prophet Isaiah reminds us in, (Isaiah 5:11) (TLB) "Look to the rock from which you were hewn, and to the quarry from which you were dug." By recognizing that everyone has to overcome sinful errors, we are less prone to boast proudly of our own humble achievements.

(James 4:10) (KJV) "Humble yourselves in the sight of the Lord, and He shall lift you up." (Psalm 69:32) (KJV) "The humble shall see this and be glad; and you who seek God, your hearts shall live."

# "Honesty"

We all prefer to be among honest people..... People you feel have earned your trust. People who will not lie, be dishonest. People who don't try to intentionally deceive us.

A noble goal for one's life is to pursue honesty-honesty with others, honesty with ourselves, and honesty with God. Honesty is the best policy. The Bible tells us, "The truth shall make you free."

Honesty can leave us to be attacked by dishonest people. Some dishonest people tend to hide their dishonesty well. Though it may be hard to be honest all the time, if we do it with loving intentions, the burden that dishonesty brings will be lifted.

Honesty is more than not telling lies. It begins inside us with our own motives and moves outward to how we deal with others. What we do when we lie is exposed and determines our level of honesty. An honest person sincerely desires to face up to their lies and get back to honesty.

It's sometimes hard to face others with the truth and deal with the consequences. But if we keep the truth concealed, we will always pay the price. How small a thing, like honesty, will ruin or save a person.

We are all capable of dishonesty. Even Jesus' close friend lied when he was under pressure and his life seemed in danger. Later though, he traveled around boldly proclaiming the truth. Honesty is a very important trait in God's eyes. He detests lying so much. No legacy is so rich as is honesty.

Being honest with our feelings is very difficult to some people, but dishonesty builds walls that can be difficult to tear down. When we are honest with others about how we feel, we are drawn closer together. Honesty in any relationship is important to keep a relationship together.

It is not always easy to be honest when confronted by another. Many times we know they may not want to hear the truth. Yet if we want a relationship to grow, honesty is fertile soil.

George Washington once wrote in a letter to Alexander Hamilton, in 1788, "I hope I shall always possess firmness and virtue enough to maintain what I consider the most enviable of all titles, the character of an 'Honest Man.'"

Solomon's wisdom about honesty, (Proverbs 12:13) (NLB) "Lies will get any man into trouble, but honesty is our own defense." (Proverbs 12:14) (NLB) "Telling the truth gives a man great satisfaction." (Proverbs 12:17) (NLB) "A good man is known for truthfulness, a false man by deceit and lies." (Proverbs 12:19) (NLB) "Truth stands the test of time, lies are soon exposed."

Honesty begets honesty. Honest people bring forth honest children.

# "Kindness"

We've heard that "action speaks louder than words." And so it is with Christian life. Like it or not, we effect others by what we say and do. The Bible tells us in, (Proverbs 3:3) (NLT) "Never time of loyalty and kindness. Hold these virtues tightly." The Bible also says in, (Colossians 3:12) (NIV) "Clothe yourselves with compassion, kindness, humility, gentlness, and patience." Whether with friends, family, coworkers or total strangers, God wants us to always treat others with the utmost care and respect.

In response to all God has done for us, let us outdo each other in being helpful and kind to each other, and in doing good. Always set a high value on spontaneous kindness. He whose inclination prompts him to cultivate one's friendship of his own accord will love and respect you more than one in whom you have been in disagreement.

We often do not get a second chance for doing good that we should have done in the first place. So if you're lucky enough to get a second chance to do good, do it now. When our lives have been changed by God's mercy, we are expected to show this same kind of mercy in our dealings with others.

Just one seemingly simple act of kindness can have far-reaching effects. If we stop to help someone out, we might make their day, or even make a new friend. Remember, what goes around, comes around. Do unto others as you would want them to do unto you.

(Luke 6:35) (NIV) "But love your enemies, do good to them, and lend to them without expecting to get anything back. Then your reward will be great, and you will be called sons of the most High. Therefore, we are admonished to pray for people rather than to insult them, pay them back, or get even with them.

A friend is a person with whom I may be honest and sincere with.

11

Before him I may speak aloud. A friend is the first person who comes when the whole world has gone out. Treat your friends for what you know them to be. Consider not what they did, but what they intend to do. We ought to help one another by our advice, and yet more by our good example.

Be kind to others and they will more than likely be kind to you. And if that doesn't work, theres always that old saying, 'kill them with kindness.'

# "Integrity"

When we think of someone with integrity we tend to think of a person who is trustworthy. A person that shows honorable intentions. To be a person called one with integrity, is a high compliment. Such a person knows the importance of doing right. Jesus provides the best example of a man with integrity; He was not swayed by influences of others, but lived a life of righteousness.

We prize integrity above other tangible things of life. Most people are concerned about being what we say we are. To become a person of high integrity is worth pursuing.

A person of integrity concerns himself not just with doing right, but also in having the right motives. Many view saying, "I was wrong," or, "I need help," as a sign of being weak. But when we can admit our weakness is when we begin to show our true strength.

Parents instill integrity in their children, not by what they say, but more by what they do. Such organized groups, like Cub Scouts and Brownies, also assist in teaching our children integrity, so that they will grow up honorably. Our honor and our good name, along with our reputation, is dependent on our integrity.

God desires us to act honorably, desiring that we do right, even if no one is watching. When others refuse to do right, we should take up the banner of integrity by doing the right thing. People of integrity keep the promises they make. They are true to their word whether in buisiness, family life, or in their relationship with God.

A person in a position of leadership that shows integrity, people tend to take notice. This provides the perfect time point out to them, that your integrity comes from God. 'How far that little candle throws it's beam! So shines a good deed in a naughty world.'

13

Often times, when we try to do the right thing, there are many oppositions. It is a test of our integrity. We must stand firm. It is one thing to say, "I believe this is the right action." It's quite another to do the right thing when we are opposed by others.

It is not true that people of integrity don't get tested. They often do. They are just more ready for any test, and they know how to handle it. No one said that having integrity was going to be easy. Often it's a strain, but if you keep strong in your belief, in the end it will be worth the struggle.

# "Wisdom"

The bible urges us to "Acquire Wisdom, Acquire Understanding!" (Proverbs 4:5) (KJV). We are instructed to gain knowledge. Wisdom-knowing the difference from truth or false. Knowing and doing right - and having common sense is a big part of what defines wisdom.

Wisdom is the ability to meet each situation with discernment and good judgement, whether dealing with others, making tough choices, or dispensing of justice. Wisdom involves using knowledge that we obtain, to take the proper course of action.

We all want to do something effective in this world while we are here. The key is being faithful to what God lay's on our hearts. God's highest priority is that we get to know Him and live a life that reflects His love and justice. When did you last pause to recognize God's wisdom in the timing of events in your life? Have you thanked Him?

Having knowledge is not the same as having wisdom. The true test of wisdom is knowing how and when to act. Wisdom is a virtue which enables each of us to make decisions. To put it in layman's terms, a wise man is one who can solve his problems.

If you seek God's wisdom, the key is being faithful to what God lay's on your heart. When we allow Christ to influence our thoughts, He becomes the source of our wisdom. He will guide us to make wise decisions and to act on them.

Throughout the ages, men that held the highest office of the United States have gotten their wisdom from the highest authority of all. Past presidents, such as George Washington, Ulysses S. Grant, Calvin Coolidge, Herbert Hoover, even Jimmy Carter, all profess to have acquired their wisdom from the pages of God's word. From a wise man comes careful and pursuasive speech.

(Proverbs 4:5-7) (KJV) "Get wisdom, get understanding, forget it not; neither decline from the words from my mouth. Forsake her not and she shall preserve thee: love her and she shall keep thee. Wisdom is the principal thing; therefore get wisdom and with thy getting get understanding."

Growing in wisdom means growing in love, tolerance, grace and acceptance. (Daniel 12:3) (NTB) "And those who are wise - the people of God - shall shine as brightly as the sun's brillance, and those who turn many to righteousness will glitter like stars forever."

# "Peace"

Peace describes the state we all long for. The word 'peace' is an emotion of calm and quiet, freedom from disturbing thoughts or emotions, an agreement to end war. It evokes images of people getting along with each other, and living together in harmony. A similar sense comes from inner peace: a quality of inner calm and rest. Neither form of peace can be had without a price. We must let go of our turmoil, and let God have control of our emotions and our thoughts. Only then can we obtain true peace.

God wants us to know peace in every area of our lives - peace in our daily work, our business, our family, our soul. The key to allowing peace to enter in us, is to invite God into each of those areas in our lives, starting with our soul. We pray for peace and an end to war and conflict. But because when we're not in control of this, we must ask and rely on God to overtake war so that He can promote His peace.

(2 Peter 3:14) (TLB) "Peace-Serene, confidence, free from fear and agitation passions and moral conflict." One of the greatest peace - robbers in our lives is anger. It effects our minds as well as our emotions. If we choose to let go of it, with God's help, we can obtain and embrace real peace. (Romans 12:18) (NIV) "If it is possible as far as it depends on you, live at peace with everyone."

If we want to have peace with others, we need to let loose of those things that are self serving. Only then can we truly achieve peace. To have peace with others, we need to find peace from within ourselves, for true peace to be possible. (Matthew 5:9) (NIV) "Blessed are the peacemakers; for they shall be called the children of God." We won't find peace from pills or therapy. It is true peace that comes from God alone.

(Proverbs 16:7) (KJV) "When a man's ways are pleasing to the Lord,

He makes even his enemies live at peace with him." If we really want peace the way God views peace, God is always ready to give us true peace.

When we focuss on the negative, peace has a way to elude us. But possitive thoughts lead to peace. Instead of lugging around our cares, we can pray. Prayer opens the door for peace. The soul celebrates when war ends whether on the battlefields, in our homes, on the job, or inside each one of us. At those times, peace is a most welcome site indeed. Remember peace brings about peace.

# "GENEROSITY"

We all have a number of resources from which to share with others. Having a 'generous spirit' does not mean simply giving money. Time is most certainly a precious commodity. Generous volunteers enable an organization to function well. It takes people generously volunteering their time to make things happen. Places such as hospitals, missions, nursing homes, animal shelters, and the list goes on, all use generous people volunteering time.

What talents/gifts do you have to share? It does not take much to be generous. Sometimes just taking time to listen is a form of generosity. A 'generous spirit' means openly giving of ones time to help another. Great is the reward of the person who generously gives whatever they have to help others.

God loves a cheerful giver. True faith is demonstrated when we look for ways to be kind and generous to those in need. (Proverbs 11:24) (KJV) "One man gives freely, yet grows all the richer; another withholds what he should give, and only suffers wants." (Acts 20:35) (NIV) "It is more blessed to give, than to recieve."

The bible lets us know that giving a small amount generously is much more important than giving a large amount grudgingly. (Proverbs 11:25) (KJV) "A generous man will prosper; he who refreshes others will himself be refreshed."

Edward Everett Hale wrote these words to encourage us to give generously; I am only one, but still I am one. I cannot do everything, but still I can do something; and because I cannot do everything, I will not refuse to do something that I can do."

"See what love the Father has given that we shall be called the children of God." We won't find peace from pills or therapy. It is true peace that comes from God alone.

(Proverbs 16:7) (KJV) "When a mans ways are pleasing to the Lord, He makes enven his enemies live at peace with him." If we really want peace the way God views peace, God is always ready to give us true peace.

When we focuss on the negative, peace has a way to elude us. But possitive thoughts lead to peace. Instead of lugging around our cares, we can pray. Prayer opens the door for peace. The soul celebrates when war ends whether on the battlefields, in our homes, on the job, or inside each one of us. At those times, peace is a most welcome site indeed. Remember peace brings about peace.

# "Joy"

What a joy it has been for me to be able to use my gift of writing to put this book together. I charge my gift to spread joy to others, because of my Lord and Savior.

When we think of joy, the words happy, love, new, and God come to mind. Lets take these words and see how they connect to joy.

Happy people smile alot. Happiness brings laughter to the soul. True joy goes beyond happiness. We all want to be happy, but joy goes much deeper than just being happy.

People who love, have joy. To love someone or something, is to bring joy to ones heart. Finding new love makes us feel joyful.

When a child opens a new toy on Christmas day, they are filled with joy. Each new day brings excitement and joy of the unknown. A newborn brings parents such joy.

God gave us all the joy of life. We rejoice in God's miracles. Sing a joyful noise unto the Lord. The joy of the Lord is with us.

When we experience true joy, we will naturally express our joy. As God pours joy into our lives, we can send up joy back to him. (Philippians 4:4) (KJV) "Rejoice in the Lord always; again, I will say rejoice!" (1 Peter 1:8) (TLB) "Though now you do see Him, yet believing, you rejoice with joy and full of glory."

Cultures throughout the world have used drums to express joy. During certain festivals, rituals and ceremonies, dance was part of the way they showed their joy and beliefs. Dancing is done at feasts, concerts, and weddings to show joy.

It's wonderful to watch a person show joy freely. We long to give ourselves permission to express joy. Laughter is such a part of joy. Joy is contagious. The return of laughter brings back such renewed joy.

It seems whatever brings us the greatest joy, also brings us sorrow. Every mother knows that. We would not feel sorrow if we never felt joy. We can maintain joy when we remember how faithful our God is. Focusing on him brings such renewed joy.

There is great joy in finding things that we have lost. Sometimes we lose our joy, like the older son of the prodigal son. The good news is that we can turn to God to find our joy again.

How wonderful it is that God wants us to experience the joy of His love, as He allows us to pursue happiness and enjoy His joy. Joy is the inner celebration that nothing on the outside can change, the fact that God loves each of us.

It has been a true joy sharing these thoughts with each of you. My prayer is that you find joy in this life and in God's word.

Dear Uncle Stuart, here are some of the poems that I wrote. I hope you enjoy them.

"Think Up"

Whenever you're down, think up!
Let a rainbow color your dreams.
Remember, love lifts each day,
And makes life more than it seems.

Whenever you're down, think up!
Let your lips keep a curve of a smile.
You'll see hopes bright rays,
And joy put flight to each day's trial.

Whenever you're down, think up!
 God's sunlight will banish gloom.
  When the spirit is happy all is well,
   And fear has no place in this room.

# WHENEVER YOU ARE...I WILL

Whenever you're sad, I will dry your tears.
   Whenever you're scared, I will comfort your fears.
   When you need love, My heart I will share.
When you are sick, for you I will care.
   When you are worried, I will give you hope.
   When you are confused, I will help you cope.
When you are lost and can't see the light,
My love will be a beacon shining so bright.

And when you stumble, and fall down in the sand,
   I will pick you up, and forever hold your hand.
   Give Me all your worries, pain, and your fears,
For you My children there is nothing I will not bear.
   I shed My blood on the cross, so you may live.
   This is My gift, that I freely give.
Keep Me in your heart, for I will always be true.
And remember this always, that I truly love you!

**SMILE ☺, God Loves You!**

By Don Brush, Suwannee Corrections, Fl.

# TEMPTED BEHIND THE FENCE

Incarceration sometimes breeds temptation-for myself anyway. Most of the time temptation leads to sin, and it separates us from God. So, how do I deal with temptations in my confined life?

Tempt and temptation may at times have the meaning "enticement to sin." Proverbs has some fine examples; "If sinners entice you, do not consent" (Prov. 1:10 RTV), or "A man of violence entices his neighbor" (Prov. 16:29 RBT). Did you notice the application here? But the words' main idea and overriding meaning is that of "testing the worth and character" of men, and sometimes of God. Let's think of a test like this; "A challenge which God might bring our way to prove the strength of our faith" (W.B.D.P. 1678).

When God asked Abraham to offer his only son, Isaac, as a sacrifice, he was "testing" the sincerity of Abraham's trust in Him (Heb. 11:17). David cried out, "Test me, O Lord (Ps 26:2), try me and know my thought (Ps. 139:23). God also told Jeremiah, "I test the mind (Jer.17:10), like one refining silver (Prov. 17:3 RTB this paragraph).

As noted in Psalm 139:23 and Jeremiah 17:10, God is looking at, or testing the heart – mind. In Romans 12:2 Paul then says, "Don't copy the behavior and customs of this world, but let God transform you into a new person" by "changing the way you think" (NLT), "the renewing of your mind" (KJV).

And remember, when you are being tempted, do not say, "God is tempting me." God is never tempted to do wrong, and He never tempts anyone else. Yet Paul said that temptation comes from our mind; our own desires which entice us and drag us away from God. These desires give birth to sinful actions. And when sin is allowed to grow, it gives birth to death and separation from our Lord (James 1:13-15 HLT).

So, what's a person to do with temptation on a daily basis? We must rely on the promises of God in 1 Corinthians 10:13, "The temptations in your life are no different from what others experience. And God is faithful. He will not allow the temptation to be more than you can stand. When you are tempted, He will show you a way out so that you can endure" (NLT).

When God laid on my heart to quit smoking cigarettes some 20 years ago; behind the fence no less, I was fit to be tied. Cigarettes had been a large part of me from my early teens, and I loved smoking. In prison I was born again I suffered ridicule from other Christians because I smelled like smoke. One day God took the butts from me and tossed them into a dumpster. Then my "so called" friends became upset because they could no longer bum-a=rip from me. Yet I kept reaching into my shirt pocket, a force of habit.

I began to carry a pocket Bible where the rip used to be. When I felt the urge to puff-a-little, I reached into my pocket and retrieved the little Bible, and read a couple of Psalms. It took about as much time to read a little of God's word as it did to roll-a-rip and smoke it. One day I discovered my little Bible was missing, and the need for tobacco had vanished. Praise God!

To apply my experience, no matter what, just remember the temptation of Jesus in Matthew 4:1-11. Just say "NO"! The scriptures say, you must not test the Lord your God, you must only serve Him.

Toss it into the dumpster, then the tempter will go away, and the angels will take care of you. That's what the Bible says, give it up. Amen. By Dr. Kenny Johnson, Union Corrections, FL.

NLT= New Life Translation of the Bible, RBT=Roget's Thesaurus of the Bible, WBD=Wycliffe Bible Dictionary

You By My Side:

The day is early,
The sun is bright,
Having you by my side,
Just feels so right.
My love for you,
Is so very real,
It's easy to show you,
Just how I feel.
Having you next to me,
Always makes me smile,
I can't stop thinking about you,
Even for a little while.
Knowing that you love me,
Knowing we'll never be apart,
You will always be my best friend,
I love you with all my heart!

Love,

## Angel On My Shoulder

There's an angel on my shoulder,
Though I never hear her sing.
I know she keeps me safe each day,
And close beneath her wing.

My angel does not play a harp,
Nor rest in clouds all day.
She's much too busy guarding me,
Keeping me from harm's way.

She rejoices in my life's success,
And weeps when I'm in pain.
She picks me up when I have fallen,
And helps me try again.

Tonight I'll say a prayer for her,
And thank the good Lord above,
For sending me an angel,
To guide me with her love!

John 14:27
Psalm 91:11

Remember a time when I was young,
The happy times, I loved to play.
Now those times are long gone past,
I now live life just for today.
We try to live a righteous life,
The Bible says No man is righteous no
not one.
But if we diligently seek Him as Lord,
He will gladly call us His son.
Each of us has a God given talent,
Be it a singer's voice or a word of praise
Or words of encouragement or words
in a poem,
It's a gift to use all our life long days.
It's God's gift to you that brings Him joy,
His gift of the singers praising song,
Keep His sermons strong, encourage all
A praise in a poem, you won't go wrong.

## God's Indescribable Gift

# AA's One Day At A Time --
# Donald L. Brush, III, Florida

When I was young and in my prime,
I used to get drunk all of the time.
Now I'm older and have more sense,
I use AA as my defense.

Drinking cuz you're lonely, Drinking cuz you're sad,
Drinking cuz you're scared, Drinking cuz you're mad;
There are so many excuses for why we drink,
If only we would take time to think.

Drinking was fun when we were young at heart,
Looking back now we wish we'd never start.
So remember how your drinking caused a crime,
Try to do it AA's way -- One Day At A Time.

You will be happier and start to smile,
You will have new friends with every mile.
You will feel better about being you,
You will find life more fun to do.

With AA you will find a friend,
Who will stick with you to the end.
Participate in AA, don't be a mime,
You'll soon be living it -- One Day At A Time.

# HELP FOR THE ADDICTS BEGINS:

Help for the addicts begins only when we are able to admit complete defeat. This can be so frightening, but it is the foundation on which we have built our lives. Most of us have tried everything we can think of, exerted every ounce of force possible, to fill the spiritual hole inside us. Nothing - not drugs, not control and management, not sex, money, property, power, or prestige - has filled it. We are powerless, our lives are unmanageable. At least by ourselves alone. Our denial will not change that fact. So we surrender, we ask our Higher Power to care for our will and our lives. Sometimes in surrendering, we don't know that a power greater than ourselves exists which can restore us to wholeness. Sometimes we're not sure that the God of our understanding will care for our unmanageable life. Our lack of certainty, though, does not effect the essential truth; We are powerless and our lives are unmanageable. We must surrender. Only by doing so can we open ourselves wide - wide enough for our old ideas and past wreckage to be cleared, wide enough for a Higher Power to enter.

Just for today: I will surrender unconditionally. I can make it as easy or as hard as I choose. Either way, I will do it!

# "REJECTION"

The pain of rejection is real, wether young or old. Young children may feel rejected by a parent. An old man may feel rejected by his children. Being rejected by loved ones hurt no matter how old you are.

But the Lord said, (Isaiah 41:10-13) "Don't be afraid, for I am with you. Do not feel dismayed (feel rejected), for I am your God. I will strengthen you. I will help you, I will uphold you with my victorious right hand. I am your Lord, your God. And I say unto you, 'Do not be afraid. I am here to help you.'"

What a wonderful God we serve. He not only loves us, but He commanded His Angels to watch over us. (Psalm 91:11). That in itself is a real comfort. But He does so much more. He cares enough for each of us. He pours out His blessings down upon us. He hears our cries. He shines His light, so we may find our way. He sent His Son to die, so we may live.

God takes our storms and turns them into victories. He has promised to be with us through all our heartbreaks, pain, temptations, loneliness, and whatever we may face in life. He has promised to be with us everyday and never leave nor forsake us. He comforts us by adding strength, encouragement, and hope with our hardships.

The Best Way
To Cheer
Yourself Up
Is To Cheer
Someone Else Up!

Love For Mom

To you Mom I send you my love,
You deserve more than I can give.

You gave me strength when I was weak,
You made my life worthy, to live.

You have been a friend when I was alone,
You are the teacher of all that I learn.

You are my comfort when I'm scared,
You give me love that's easy to earn.

I don't know what to do when you're away,
I don't know how to act while we're apart.

I only know you make my world complete,
And I give you my love with all my heart!

I love You, Mom!

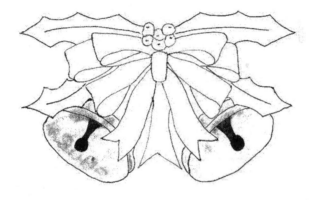

# Here's To You Dad

You raised me well, you taught me right:
"Hold your money, always be tight.
Hold your head up, you'll always go far,
And remember to be just who you are.

"Grow up like me, big and strong,
Show some patience, you won't go wrong.
Choose your friends well, stay on top of
the game,
You'll come out winning, and not be lame.

"Find a good woman, you will go far."
With this advice, I'll be like you are.
I'll remember this wisdom, as it was
told,
I'll remember you Dad, and always be
bold.

I Love You Dad,

Your Son!

# Family Love

The love of family is precious indeed,
When you're lonely or in need.

No matter that you're behind bars.
When you hear from them, you float like
stars.

You always pray they're doing their best,
When you get a letter, you feel blessed.

Hearing from family really picks you up,
Your spirit is lifted and filled is your cup.

Love your family, always be true,
Your life will fill with joy and never be
blue.

I'm so thankful for my family love,
Like Angels keeping me safe from above.


God Bless My Family Love

# "Solemn Vow"

There is one vow I pray to keep,
May everything I say and do,
Dear Lord, be pleasing in Your sight,
And reflect my love for You.

And no matter where life takes me,
As I'm walking down life's bumpy road,
Let me help a friend in need,
And share someone's heavy load.

No matter what turn this road leads,
May what I do for others be,
On any given single day,
What I would have them do for me.

Through all my ups and all my downs,
May I show them kindness every day,
No matter who I may meet,
To everyone who comes my way.

And dear Lord please,
Walk beside me now,
And help me keep,
This Solemn Vow.

# To: Uncle Stuart & Aunt Laura;

## What My God Has Done For Me:

He is the all powerful, He is my Master.
He is the true 'I AM', He is my healer.
He is my Father. He is my friend.
He is all that I need, He is my God.

When darkness befalls me, He will shine a light.
When I'm scared, He will hold my hand.
When I'm lost, He will show me the way.
When I'm lonely, He will sooth my soul.

He is the one, that lives within me.
He is the one, that fills my thoughts.
He is the one, that I can turn to.
He is the one, that I can truly trust.

Now that I know Him, I'm never in darkness.
Now that I know Him, I'm never afraid.
Now that I know Him, I shall alway's find my way.
Now that I know Him, my soul is filled with joy.

Chorus
I thank Him, for His sacrifice.
I thank Him, for His tolerence.
I thank Him, for His forgivness.
I thank my God, for His love.

Written by D.L. Brush III

# TIME FOR A CHANGE

When I was young and in my prime,
There was a devastation in my life, all the time.
My life was a wreck, no matter where I go,
Everyone who saw me, would surely know.

Day after day, my life was filled with gloom.
It seemed my life was surely headed for doom.
I hated my life, with nowhere to turn.
I was looking for joy, that I desperately yearn.

I lost everything I had, my home and my wife.
I felt so alone; I just wanted to end my life.
I was feeling so bad, at the end of my rope,
Felt like I had no chance, I had no hope.

As I lay in my sadness, at the bottom of a pit,
With my eyes closed, I saw a light that was lit.
A voice filled my head, an angel I heard in my ears:
"Pray to Him," the voice said, "He will stay near."

So I asked for forgiveness, as I began to cry,
I don't know how, and I don't know why.
My burdens were lifted, right off of me,
I began to feel hope, now I was free.

Free from the hatred, that I kept inside,
My spirit lifted, I had no reason to hide.
God showed mercy, with His forgiven love,
As He sent to me, His angel from above!

# GOD HAS PERFORMED A MIRACLE ON ME;

God has performed a miracle on me,
He has lifted me up and set me free.
His loving mercy is all I need,
He has lifted me up and set me free.

My God has shone me mercy, My God shows me love.
He has sent me an angel, to watch over me from above.
God has forgiven me, of all my past sins,
He has washed my soul clean, from deep within.

Now I rejoice, and bless His holy name,
To know that I am healed, and no more am I lame.
Thank you my God, for sending your angel to me,
And for fulfilling your loving promise, that at last has set me free.

So when your feeling lonely, down in despair,
Trust in God's loving mercy, He will shed all your fear.
Let God have all your problems, and keep your faith true,
God has a plan for you, if you just remember that God truly loves you!

## No Other

You are my beautiful 'Rose,'
My sweet smelling flower.
I love you more and more each day,
With every passing hour.

You are the sunshine,
That lights up my life.
I could not be more pleased,
That I chose you to be my wife.

You bring me joy and happiness,
With every passing day.
Word could not possibly express,
The passion for you I want to say.

I love you with all my heart,
Like a child loves his mother.
God made you for me,
For me there is no other!

**Valentine's Day**

# ANNIVERSARIES;

A date like no other day, when two people come together to confess their love for each other. A day that binds two people through love and passion. A day to remind yourselves of why you both came together in the first place. A day to show each other what love is really all about. A day to reflect on the good memories that you've shared. A day to contemplate your future happiness. A day ever reminding you both that God's love joined you both together for loving goodness. To my (wife/husband) I profess my love to you for all the rest of my days. May God's love keep you both together through life's journey. May this day bring happy thoughts of your precious love that you both share together!

# PRAYER GROUPS

Good News!! We have a Prayer Group in
our dorm. Sometimes ten inmates come to
pray. We lift up each other as well as our
families. It's truly a blessing.

There are a lot of good things that are now
happening at Suwanee C.I. I have seen
so many inmates get baptized here. And a
lot of inmates attend Church services. It is
good to see our brotherhood in Christ grow.

I made my request known to our Chaplain
that I would like to be a Chaplain's Orderly.
We have a good Chaplain here and an Assistant
Chaplain as well. We have a great
Praise Team. I gave my songs to the Praise
Team -- they are going to put music to them.

       Your Nephew, A Child in Christ

# DESTINY

We often think that holding on makes us strong, but sometimes true strength is found in letting go. Letting go of what we want, all of our assumptions and preconceptions, allows us to accept an infinitely wider view of life.

It's not what is happening to us now, or what happened to us in the past, that makes us what we become. Rather our decision about what to focus on that determines our ultimate destiny!

**"UNTIL"**

I never dreamed one smile could
Fill my days with warmth and light,
Until your smile made my whole world
So beautiful and bright.

I never realized someone could
Change my life so much,
Until you shared your caring ways,
Your strength and your tender touch.

I never thought that love could be
So endless, deep and true,
Until the day that I gave
My heart and my love to you!

I Love You Soo Much!

With All My Love,

Thank you for your service theme. We get credit for one card that we do, but are able to make several, if we wish. I made a total of 10 cards, to spread joy, for our veterans. Each one is different. I wrote two poems for them. I'll write my military poems down for you to share with any veterans you come across.

### 'For Your Bravery'

You served your country bravely,
Your a hero in our heart.
It's men and women just like you,
That sets this nation apart.

We thank you for your service,
And your sacrifices you bare.
For your bravery in the field,
Our pride for you we share.

### To The Heroes Of Our Nation

Your service to this great nation,
Is appreciated more than words can say.
Because of your sacrifice we remain free,
Your a hero of yesterday and still a hero today.

Your bravery can't be measured by a ruler,
Or a yardstick, nor even a measuring tape.
Your a super hero of our people,
Without a colorful costume or a fancy cape.

Your a patriot for our country,
Your the reason we remain free.
Your the hero of the United States,
And all her mini me's.

My Prayer To God:

Dear Heavenly Father,
I humbly stand before you like an
open book. Because you know every
word that I say before I say it.
Because you know every act that I do
before I act it. Because you know every
thought I think before I think it.
Because you know every deed that I've done
before I did it. I thank you for
Your loving forgiveness. And I ask
You to help me be a shining light
for others. Help me to strengthen the
ties that bind the good in me to be
a help to others.

In Jesus' name I pray,
    Amen...

10/16

# 'What Is The Meaning Of Life?'

The meaning of life has many different meanings to different people. We could write a book on the meaning of life. There are such books.

To most people the meaning of life is to be wealthy and healthy. To some it's just being happy.

Some people have selfish reasons for living. While others just don't care about life at all.

Some people are created to be a family oriented person. Some were meant to be alone. Some were created to be Mothers and Fathers. While some were meant to stay single.

One thing is for certain we were all created to die. No one that is born will live forever, though some would like to think so.

In conclusion, the meaning of life is up to each individual person. God gave us a free will. It is how we use our time here on earth that determines how meaningful our life becomes.

For those who live life to destoy and deceive others, they live a pretty meaningless life. Which means when their life is over, no one will remember them.

For those who live life for the good of others, their life will have a meaning. People will remember those who do good.

It does not matter rather you do good or not. At the end of it all, we will all judged by our maker. May each of us find mercy in His Grace!

The purpose of life is to get ready for life above the sun.

# "Let Us Rejoice"

When we think of the word rejoice, we generally think about happy occasions, such as weddings, the birth of a child. This calls for a celebration. A party filled with food, friends, dancing, and plenty of laughter.

When we go to church and sing hymns, we are singing praises to the Lord. We are in fact rejoicing. When we get baptized, the whole church rejoices with us. All around the world people celebrate and rejoice for a New Year.

The most important reason to rejoice is the birth of our Lord Jesus Christ. On the day that Baby Jesus was born, the angels did rejoice. (Luke 2:13, 14, NKJV) "And suddenly there was with the angel a multitude of the heavenly host praising God and saying; 'Glory to God in the highest, And on earth peace, good will toward men!' And when the three wise men saw the star in the east; (Matthew 2:10, NKJV) 'When they saw the star, they rejoiced with exceedingly great joy.'"

As we pray and give thanks to the Lord we rejoice in Him. (Psalm 33:1, NKJV) "Rejoice in the Lord, O you righteous! For praise from the upright is beautiful." We should alway give the Lord thanks for what he does for us. (Psalm 63:7; NKJV) "Because you have been my help, therefore in the shadow of your wings I will rejoice."

We not only rejoice here on earth, but the heavens also rejoice. (Psalm 97:1, NKJV) "The Lord reigns; Let the eart rejoice." (Psalm 96:11, NKJV) "Let the heavens rejoice, and let the earth be glad."

Paul tells us to rejoice in the Lord all the time. (Philippians 4:4, NKJV) "Rejoice in the Lord always. Again I say Rejoice!" (Psalm 18:24, NKJV) "This is the day that the Lord has made; We will rejoice and be glad in it!"

Now that I feel better, I'm gonna copy down this poem I wrote. I hope you enjoy it.

# HOMEWARD BOUND

We have heard it said, "Home is where the heart is."
Dorothy, from the Wizard of Oz, made this quote
famous -- "There's no place like home." In the song, 'Papa
was a rolling stone,' We hear the next line say,
"Where he lay his hat was his home. Yet another quote
is the American logo, "Home, Sweet Home."

The definition of a home is: A structure so that people
have a shelter in which to live. There are many styles
of homes -- a house, a trailer, an apartment, a tent, even
a park bench. Any of these could suffice. Cavemen
made their homes in caves. Indians used tepees, wig-
wams, and lean-tos.

Even animals have homes: Bears arrange their
furniture in caves. Rabbits and rodents dig holes in the
ground. Turtles carry their homes on their backs.

(Psalm 84:3, NKJV) "Even the sparrow has found a
home, and the swallow a nest for herself, where she
lay her young." The owl's family looks out from a
hollow in a tree.

But now, where is God's home? In Heaven? Is the
Church the House of God? Or the Cathedral, Synagogue,
or Chapel? Or all of the above? These all are
known as the House of God.

And when we die, where do we go? (2 Corinthians 5:1, NKJV "For we know if our earthly house, this tent, is destroyed, we have a building from God, a house not made with hands, eternal and in the Heavens."

Jesus spoke of God's Heavenly home. (John 14:2 NKJV, NKJV) "In my Father's house are many mansions; if it were not so, I would have told you. I go to prepare a place for you." Can you imagine Jesus as the carpenter building a home for you in Heaven?? Keep the praises of Jesus in your heart, and let His strength carry you HOMEWARD BOUND!

(D.L.B.)

# HEAVENLY THOUGHTS

Thoughts of Heaven, puts my mind at ease,
God's wonderful kingdom, fills my heart with please.
Pearly Gates and streets of gold,
Knowing that no one really grows old.

Knowing that His love, has set me free,
He has opened my eyes, now I can see.
His loving mercy, it will never end,
My prayers of thanks, to him I send.

He has seen me through, some pretty tough time
I'm filled with joy, and peace is mine.
He has given me joy, and peace of mind,
Just one simple prayer, He's never hard to find.

Well I got a little ahead of myself. But I hope that you enjoy the poem.
May God continue his healing powers for you and Aunt Laura. I look
forward to your next letter. My love and best wishes for you all.

In The Spirit Of Christ,
Your Nephew
Don

John 14:12

Peace I leave with you,
My peace I give you.
I do not give to you as the world
gives.
Do not let your heart be
troubled,
And do not be afraid.

# BIBLIOGRAPHY

Treasury of God's virtues (1999) by Elaine Wright Colvin & Elaine Creasman. Published by Publications International, Ltd.

Holy Bible (New International Version) (2010). Published by American Bible Society

Holy Bible (King James Version) (1985). The Gideons International

Holy Bible (The Living Bible) (1971.) Tyndale House Pubishers

Printed in the United States
By Bookmasters